Never Skip Dessert!

by Elaine Acker

ISBN: 979-8-9859979-1-0 (Paperback)

Original & licensed stock images are provided by the author.

This book was created using a proprietary publishing platform, The Cookbook Creative. All content is the sole responsibility of the author. The Cookbook Creative is responsible for production, printing, & distribution only.

The Cookbook Creative
a Division of Sparx360
2121 Lohman's Crossing Road
Suite 504 Box 269
Austin, TX 78734

TheCookbookCreative.com

To Katherine Acker, AKA Mama
For filling the kitchen with irresistible goodies &
warm memories that will last a lifetime.

And to the Acker Family
This family is the gift that keeps giving! I'm grateful for you
(& your recipes!) every single day!

TABLE OF CONTENTS

"The story of your favorite foods is your culinary memoir, not a nameless collection of recipes..."

Chef Edward Lee

Introduction

Whether you're a professional chef or the keeper of treasured family recipes, chances are, your favorite memories were made in the kitchen, just like mine.

I wrote this book because in our house, dessert was the most important meal of the day. Or something like that. Mama always made sure Daddy had a fresh dessert waiting after every evening meal. I wasn't big on sweets, but if it was something she thought I might eventually want (like a sliver of sweet potato pie), she'd hide a little piece in the back of the ice box. Because in our house, desserts vanished like ghosts.

Writing this book gave me a place to focus on fun memories & share favorite recipes with my cousins. And it was the best way I could think of to honor Daddy's food "point of view," which clearly was: Never Skip Dessert.

Maybe you have an idea for a cookbook, too?

I launched The Cookbook Creative because I think cookbooks are a special way to share food & stories. Whether you're creating a one-of-a-kind gift, capturing family memories, or building your food business, I want to make it easy for you to create a cookbook you'll be proud of.

Let's get started. Visit TheCookbookCreative.com & set up your account today.

I'll look forward to celebrating when you publish your book!

Sincerely,

Elaine Acker

BANANA CREAM FREEZE DESSERT MUFFINS

"Nothing finishes a dessert as simply & richly as sweetened, perfectly whipped cream. It is almost a dessert all by itself."

Roland Mesnier

There's no question that I could eat whipped cream all by itself & be perfectly content! This recipe is super easy & just calls for a frozen whipped topping. When the "muffins" are frozen, you can pop them into a freezer bag & store them for a few weeks. (If they last that long!)

Ingredients

1 cup buttermilk
½ cup sugar
4 bananas, mashed
8 ounces frozen whipped topping

Instructions

Mix ingredients & freeze in lined muffin pans. Makes 20 muffins. When frozen, remove muffins from pans & put in plastic bags in freezer.

BANANA PUDDING

"You probably wouldn't like it."

**Gerald Acker
(trying to avoid sharing the pudding)**

For some reason, this recipe reminds me of family reunions. And yes, we always hoped for pudding! If you like the cookies to stay a bit crisp, let the pudding cool completely & serve sooner rather than later. If you like the cookies with a softer, cake-like texture, layer the cookies & the pudding while the pudding is still slightly warm. They will soften even more in the refrigerator overnight.

Ingredients

2 ripe bananas
3 tablespoons of flour, heaping
¾ cup sugar
3 eggs
3 cups milk
1 teaspoon vanilla
1 tablespoon butter
1 small box of vanilla wafers

Instructions

Mix the flour & sugar with ½ cup of milk. Add eggs & mix, then add the rest of the milk. Cook over medium heat until the pudding mixture has thickened (approximately 10 minutes).

Turn off the heat & add butter & vanilla. Let the pudding cool before assembling the banana pudding by making layers of wafers & pudding.

COBBLER WITH BLACKBERRIES OR PEACHES

"Baking is done out of love, to share with family & friends, to see them smile."

Anna Olson

The very first freelance article I published in Texas Parks & Wildlife Magazine in 1992 was about Texas's abundant, sweet blackberries. And I included this recipe! I have fond memories of picking blackberries along the railroad tracks. Those days almost always ended with purple tongues & a kitchen that smelled of sweet cobbler.

Dough Ingredients

2 cups flour
½ cup shortening
⅛ teaspoon salt
½ cup water

Dough Instructions

Mix ingredients & knead. Roll out dough & cut into strips or cut into circles like biscuits. Set aside.

Filling Ingredients

2 cups blackberries or peaches
⅔ cup sugar
1 tablespoon flour
½ cup water
1 tablespoon butter
sprinkle of cinnamon

Filling Instructions

Sift sugar & flour together & put into a pan with the fruit. Sprinkle with cinnamon. Add water. Bring to a boil on medium heat. Add butter. Cook to a thick, pie-filling consistency (about 15-minutes).

Assembling the Cobbler

Preheat oven to at 350°F.

Pour cobbler filling into a 10-inch pie plate; either arrange dough strips in a checkerboard pattern across the top or place the circles of dough across the top to cover. Bake until the crust is light brown.

Serve topped with homemade vanilla ice cream.

BREAD PUDDING

"Life is uncertain. Eat dessert first."
Ernestine Ulmer

My Daddy, Gerald, & his brother Fred, both had an unwavering love for bread pudding. My cousins say that Fred's wife Dolly made bread pudding every week for him to take to work in his lunchbox. Fred preferred the version with leftover biscuits. I wonder how many times he ate the bread pudding first before he ate his lunch? Many thanks to Karen, Lisa, & Julie for sharing!

Ingredients

3 to 4 cups bread or biscuits broken into bite-sized pieces
⅔ cup sugar
2 eggs, beaten
1 tablespoon butter
3 cups hot milk
pinch salt
sprinkle nutmeg
sprinkle cinnamon
1 teaspoon vanilla
raisins, coconut, or nuts (optional)

Instructions

Preheat oven to 350°F.

Combine all ingredients except eggs in a bowl & mix. When the mixture is cool enough, add eggs & mix again. Spray a loaf pan with cooking spray & pour mixture into pan.

Bake 35 to 40 minutes until custard is set. The edges will be browned, but there will still be a small jiggle in the center of the dish.

BROWNIES & MILK

"Desserts are the fairy tales of
the kitchen—a happily-ever-after to supper."
Terri Guillemets

Daddy believed in fairy tales in the kitchen. And he found happy endings in brownies. More specifically, he loved brownies IN milk. Not with. IN. I can't really describe how this transforms the brownie experience, but you'll have to try it. It's truly the thing fairy tales are made of.

Ingredients

4 eggs
5 tablespoons cocoa
2 cups sugar
1 cup vegetable oil
1 ½ cups flour
1 teaspoon salt
2 teaspoons vanilla
1 cup chopped nuts (optional)

Instructions

Preheat oven to 350°F.

Mix all ingredients, adding nuts last. Pour into a greased & floured 9x13 pan.

Bake for 25 minutes. Do not over bake. A slightly under-done brownie is moist & creamy & perfect.

Frost with a creamy frosting. Or not. Makes about 24 large brownies.

WORLD-FAMOUS BROWNIES BY OLIVE

"It's impossible to be gloomy when you're sitting behind a marshmallow."

Charles M. Schulz

My Aunt Olive's brownie recipe is the stuff of legends. And this recipe involves marshmallows. Any reunion, Sunday dinner, funeral, or pot-luck dinner gets exponentially better when her brownies hit the table. It's one of those recipes that gets handed down over the years & nobody misplaces it. Many thanks to Polly & Mindy for sharing!

Ingredients

4 eggs
2 cups sugar
1 cup MINUS 2 tablespoons vegetable oil
1 ½ cups flour
1 teaspoon salt
1 cup nuts (optional/pecans preferred)
5 tablespoons cocoa
1 cup miniature marshmallows

Instructions

Preheat oven to 350°F.

Mix sugar, flour, salt, & cocoa in bowl. Add oil, eggs, vanilla, & nuts. Pour into a 9x13 sheet pan & bake for 30 to 35 minutes.

Immediately upon removal from the oven, place 1 cup of miniature marshmallows over the brownies, poking them down into the brownies.

Icing Ingredients

½ stick (4 tablespoons) butter
½ box powdered sugar (about 2 cups)
2 tablespoons cocoa
1 teaspoon vanilla
milk

Icing Instructions

Mix butter with powdered sugar & cocoa. Add vanilla & enough milk to make a thin icing. Pour & spread over warm brownies.

OLIVE'S THREE-LAYER CHOCOLATE CAKE

"What you see before you, my friend, is the result of a lifetime of chocolate."

Katharine Hepburn

When she wasn't baking brownies, my Aunt Olive was baking this cake, making her every bit as popular as Katharine Hepburn. It's three layers, so it's impressive. We didn't get fancy when it came to decorating, but you could do creative things with this one! Thanks to Mindy for sharing.

Ingredients:
2 ⅓ cups sugar
2 ⅓ cups flour
2 eggs
1 cup butter, softened
2 teaspoons vanilla
⅔ cup cocoa
1 cup buttermilk
2 teaspoons baking soda
1 cup boiling water
¼ teaspoon salt

Instructions:
Preheat oven to 350°F.

Cream sugar & shortening; add eggs. Mix together flour, cocoa, & salt. Add soda to buttermilk. Alternately add buttermilk & the dry ingredients to the sugar, shortening, & eggs. Add vanilla. Stir in boiling water.

Pour into 3 pans for a layered cake or use a sheet pan.

Bake for 30 to 35 minutes.

Frosting Ingredients:
1 ⅓ cup sugar
2 tablespoons cocoa
⅔ cup milk
½ stick butter (4 tablespoons)
1 teaspoon vanilla
pinch of salt

Frosting Instructions
Bring all ingredients except butter & vanilla to a soft boil. Remove from heat. Add butter & vanilla. Do not stir. Let cool & then beat until creamy & pour over cake.

CHOCOLATE CHIP CAKE

**"There is nothing better than a friend,
unless it is a friend with chocolate."**
Charles Dickens

Most of the Acker Family recipes are from scratch & I tend to turn up my nose at shortcuts. But after a while, you learn to appreciate a shortcut or two. I got this recipe from my sister Sherry & her husband JD. He was a certified bake-a-holic & tried any recipe destined for the oven. Turns out, this one was a keeper.

Ingredients:

1 box plain yellow cake mix (without pudding in the mix)
1 small box instant chocolate pudding mix
1 small box instant vanilla pudding mix
¼ cup sugar
6 ounces semi-sweet chocolate chips
1 ½ cups water
¾ cup oil
4 eggs

Instructions

Preheat oven to 350°F.

Mix all dry ingredients except chocolate chips together. Add liquid ingredients with dry ingredients until well blended. Add chocolate chips & mix gently. Pour into a greased & floured bundt pan. (You can also use plain breadcrumbs in place of flour to coat the inside of the Bundt pan to keep the cake from sticking.)

Bake 50 to 60 minutes or until a toothpick comes out clean.

CHOCOLATE CRACKLE COOKIES

"A balanced diet is having a cookie in each hand."
Barbara Johnson

It's impossible to think about Chocolate Crackle Cookies without thinking about my sister, Becky. For her, no Christmas is complete without these cookies on the table. Making a grab for a cookie can be like playing a rowdy game of spoons. You'd better be quick.

Ingredients

1 package devil's food cake
2 eggs, slightly beaten
1 tablespoon water
½ cup shortening
powdered sugar

Instructions

Preheat oven to 350°F.

Combine cake mix, eggs, water, & shortening. Mix with a spoon until it's well blended. Shape dough into balls the size of small walnuts. Dip in powdered sugar. Arrange on greased cookie sheets & bake for 8 to 10 minutes. Cool slightly & dip again in powdered sugar.

CHOCOLATE CREAM PIE

"The 12-step chocoholics program: Never be more than 12 steps away from chocolate."

Terry Moore

There was never any shortage of pie in our house: creamy fillings; lightly browned meringue on top with little brown pools of sugar. My favorite part was the meringue. Don't miss the recipes for the best pie crust on the planet & the meringue in this book.

Ingredients

1 prepared pie crust
3 tablespoons cocoa, slightly heaping
3 tablespoons flour, heaping
¾ cup sugar
3 cups milk
3 eggs, separated

Instructions

Preheat oven to 400°F.

Mix together dry ingredients. Add ½ cup of milk & 3 egg yolks. Mix well. Add remaining 2-1/2 cups of milk & cook over medium heat, stirring frequently until thickened (approximately 10 minutes). Remove from heat & add butter & vanilla.

Pour filling into a baked pie crust. Use remaining 3 egg whites to make meringue & spread over the pie.

Bake until meringue is golden brown (approximately 10 minutes).

CHOCOLATE FROSTING

"All you need is love. But a little chocolate now & then doesn't hurt."

Charles M. Schulz

This frosting is an easy go-to mixture that takes any cake to the next level of mmmmmmm.

Ingredients

3 cups powdered sugar
½ stick butter
1 teaspoon vanilla
3 level tablespoons cocoa
splash milk

Instructions

Mix all ingredients together & add splashes of milk to create a creamy texture. Frost brownies or your favorite cake.

I make this Texas Sheet Cake for company. A lot. It's a tried and true recipe that never gets old. My altruistic husband always "tests" it for our guests ahead of time, just to be sure it came out okay.

CHOCOLATE SHEET CAKE
TEXAS STYLE

"After eating chocolate, you feel godlike, as though you can conquer enemies, lead armies…"

Emily Luchetti

Ingredients:

2 cups sugar
2 cups flour
3 tablespoons cocoa
½ cup butter
½ cup shortening
1 cup water
3 eggs beaten
1 teaspoon vanilla
½ cup buttermilk
1 teaspoon baking soda

Ingredients Note:

If you don't have buttermilk on hand, just use whole milk & add 1 teaspoon of plain white vinegar. Let it sit for 2 or 3 minutes & you'll have a good substitute.

Instructions:

Preheat oven to 400°F.

Mix flour & sugar together. Put butter, cocoa, & shortening in a bowl together & melt in the microwave or in a bowl over boiling water on the stove. Add this to the sugar & flour & mix. Add the soda to the buttermilk. Let it sit for about a minute, & then add it to the flour, sugar, etc. along with the vanilla. Mix all ingredients.

Spray 9x13 baking pan with cooking spray & pour the cake mix into the pan.

Cook for about 25 minutes or until a toothpick comes out clean.

Glaze Ingredients:

¼ cup butter
1 ½ tablespoons cocoa
¼ cup milk
½ cup chopped pecans
2 cups powdered sugar
½ teaspoon vanilla

Glaze Instructions:

Bring butter, cocoa, milk, & nuts to a boil. Remove from heat & add powdered sugar & vanilla.

Mix. When cake is done, you can let it cool & then pour the glaze over cake, or you can pour it over the cake while warm & cut the cake into squares, letting the glaze melt down into the cake.

I'm not sure my Aunt Dorothy ever willingly shared her fried pies, either. They were her favorite, & Mama cooked a batch for her birthday every year. They were handmade & hand delivered in a little foil-lined box. Still warm. These require a little work, so make a big batch & keep some in the freezer.

DOROTHY'S FAVORITE FRIED PIES

"I don't share blame. I don't share credit.
And I don't share desserts."
Beverly Sills

Dough Ingredients

1 ½ cups flour
½ cup shortening MINUS
  1 tablespoon
½ teaspoon salt
4 to 5 tablespoons water

Dough Instructions

Mix together flour & salt. Cut in shortening until mixture is crumbly. Mix in 4 tablespoons of water & mix until dough forms a ball. If dough is too dry, add more water, one tablespoon at a time. Divide dough into balls & roll out on a lightly floured surface. You should have 6 crusts that measure about 6 inches in diameter. Set aside.

Filling Ingredients

6 to 8 ounces dried fruit
  of choice (peaches or
  apricots recommended)
¼ cup sugar
½ teaspoon cinnamon
water

Filling Instructions

Add fruit to a pan on the stove top & add water to cover. Cook until fruit is soft & falling apart. Pour off most of excess liquid. Add sugar & cinnamon. Adjust sugar & cinnamon to taste. Mash filling with a potato masher. Let fruit mixture cool to room temperature before assembling pies.

Assembling Pies

Place cooled fruit mixture in the center of each circle of dough. Leave clean spaces around the edges to close the pie. Moisten the edges of the dough & fold one half over the other, crimping the edges with a fork, or with your fingers.

Fry in vegetable oil over medium heat, browning both sides of each pie.

Drain on paper towels.

FUDGE PIE: QUICK CAKE IN A PIE PLATE

"Don't wreck a sublime chocolate experience by feeling guilty."

Lora Brody

Nothing could get between my high-school boyfriend & a good meal. I hadn't paid much attention to cooking back then until I realized how Mama's desserts put a smile on his face. (I'm pretty sure he was putting a frown on my Daddy's face at the same time for multiple reasons.) This was the first recipe I learned to make for him. It's easy & became very popular.

Ingredients

4 tablespoons cocoa
8 tablespoons butter
2 eggs
1 cup sugar
½ cup flour
teaspoon vanilla

Instructions

Preheat oven to 325°F.

Sift together flour & sugar. Melt together cocoa & butter. Add vanilla to cocoa & butter. Pour cocoa mixture into flour & sugar & mix. Whisk 2 eggs & add to the mixture.

Bake for approximately 20 minutes or until a toothpick comes out clean.

ITALIAN CREAM CAKE

"It takes forty muscles to frown, & only twelve to jam a cupcake in your mouth & get over it."
Sarah Ockler

So this recipe is for a cake, not a cupcake. But any cake recipe can become a cupcake with the wave of a muffin tin. This version of Mama's Italian Cream Cake has made the family news more than once. It's the recipe we turn to whenever we want to hear the word, "Wow!"

Ingredients

1 stick (½ cup) butter, softened
½ cup shortening
5 eggs, separated
2 cups sugar
1 cup buttermilk
1 cup angel flake coconut
1 tablespoons vanilla
2 cups flour
1 teaspoon soda

Instructions

Preheat oven to 350°F.

Cream butter, sugar, & shortening together. Add vanilla. Beat in egg yolks. Beat well. Stir soda into buttermilk. Alternate adding buttermilk mixture & flour to the butter, sugar, & shortening. Stir in coconut.

Beat egg whites until they form stiff peaks. Fold gently into cake mixture.

Prepare three floured & greased 9-inch cake pans. Bake for 25 minutes. DO NOT OPEN THE OVEN DOOR before the 25 minute mark.

Cool cake & assemble cake with frosting below; spread the frosting between layers & on top & sides.

Frosting Ingredients

1 (8-ounce) package cream cheese, softened
1 stick (½ cup) butter, softened
1 box (2 cups) powdered sugar
1 tablespoon vanilla
1 cup chopped nuts (pecans recommended)

Frosting Instructions

Combine all ingredients & beat until creamy.

If you love extra thick frosting, increase the frosting recipe by half.

LEMON MERINGUE PIE

"You may be given a load of sour lemons, why not try to make a dozen lemon meringue pies?"

Maya Angelou

My Aunt Dolly made this every year at Thanksgiving for my Uncle Fred & my cousins. And the tradition has lasted with cousins Karen, Lisa, & Julie. We didn't have it as often at our house I don't think Daddy really wanted to eat lemons when chocolate & vanilla were in the kitchen. But I love this pie. To me, lemon meringue pie tastes like summer.

Ingredients

1 (8 or 9 oz) pie shell, baked
3 eggs, separated
1 (14 oz) can sweetened condensed milk
½ cup lemon juice

Instructions

Preheat oven to 350°F.

In medium bowl, beat egg yolks. Stir in sweetened condensed milk & lemon juice. Pour into baked shell. Top with meringue (recipe in this book), completely covering the filling to the edge of the pie crust. Bake for 12 to 15 minutes or until meringue is golden brown.

MERINGUE

"Meringue covers a multitude of sins."
Joe Perkins

If Mama made a pie, I was right there in the kitchen with her, mostly because I wanted to play with the meringue. If you want to feel like a kid again, make a pie & put lots of little pointy peaks in the meringue.

Ingredients

3 eggs whites at room temperature
6 tablespoons sugar
¼ teaspoon cream of tartar (optional)

Instructions

Preheat oven to 350°F.

Beat 3 egg whites until frothy.

Add sugar, a little at a time, until the mixture forms stiff peaks.

Add cream of tartar to help stabilize the meringue.

Spread on your favorite pie & bake until the swirls & peaks in the meringue turn a golden color (about 10 minutes).

PECAN PIE

"Pie makes everybody happy."
Laurie Halse Anderson

Daddy spent hours cracking & shelling fresh pecans by hand, just so he could savor the flavor of Mama's pecan pie. (Sometimes, making memories takes a little hard work!) These days, buying pecans at the store makes life easier, but I'll give you bonus points if you get them from your local grower.

Ingredients:

1 pie crust
Make Katherine's Best Pie Crust Ever or pick up a pie crust at the store. Don't blind bake (pre-bake) the crust.
¾ cup sugar
2 tablespoons flour
3 eggs
5 tablespoons butter (melted)
1 teaspoon vanilla
1 cup Karo syrup (light or dark)
1 ½ cups pecan halves

Instructions:

Preheat oven to 350°F.

Mix all ingredients & pour into prepared crust. Bake for 55 minutes to an hour. When the pie is done, there will still be a tiny jiggle in the middle. It will firm up as it cools! If you want to get a little fancy, you can use leftover dough to decorate the center of the pie. Brush it with a little egg wash to make it shine.

The edges of the crust can become a toasty brown while waiting for the center of the pie to cook. If you don't like the darker brown crust, you can protect the edges with foil to prevent over-cooking.

No lie. This is the only pie crust I've ever liked. I believe with all my heart it's the best pie crust ever. So many crusts are greasy. Why??? This one is tasty & flaky & makes every pie filling better. Lots of people buy ready-made pie crusts at the store, but this one is simple & you might find a little Zen in the rolling pin.

KATHERINE'S PIE CRUST
THE BEST PIE CRUST EVER

"We must have pie.
Stress cannot exist in the presence of a pie."
David Mamet

Ingredients:
1-1/2 cups flour MINUS 1 tablespoon
½ cup shortening
1 teaspoon salt
4+ tablespoons water

Instructions:

Preheat oven to 425°F.

Mix dry ingredients. Then add water to form a dough consistency. If the dough is too dry, add more water, one tablespoon at a time, until the dough reaches the proper consistency.

Roll out on lightly floured surface, making sure the edges extend a little more than an inch in diameter beyond the width of the pie plate.

When you've rolled the dough to the proper size, roll the dough around the rolling pin, & then transfer it to the pie plate by unrolling it over the pie plate.

Crimp the edges with your fingers or finish the edge with a fork.

Bake for 15 minutes or until done.

NOTE:

Some recipes call for pie crusts to be baked (blind baked) before adding the filling. With others, you'll add the filling & then bake. Check your recipe!

PLAIN WHITE CAKE

"A party without cake is just a meeting."
Julia Child

This cake is truly a blank canvas. I can't count the number of birthday cakes that started with this simple-yet-yummy recipe. One year, I wanted a cake that looked like a castle. Mama made it happen using this cake recipe baked in a sheet pan. She baked a second one to build the castle; added sugar cones for turrets; & used squares of chocolate for doors & windows. It's still my favorite birthday cake ever.

Ingredients:
2 cups + 2 tablespoons sifted flour
3 tablespoons baking powder
1 ½ cups sugar
1 teaspoon salt
⅔ cup shortening
1 cup milk
1 ½ teaspoons vanilla
3 eggs

Instructions:
Preheat oven to 350°F.

Prepare two, 9-inch layer pans. Grease & dust with flour.

Sift together dry ingredients, including flour, baking powder, sugar, & salt; add shortening, milk, & vanilla. Beat with electric mixer for 2 minutes. Add 3 eggs & beat for another 2 minutes.

Pour into prepared pans & bake for 30 to 35 minutes until done.

Cool & finish with your favorite frosting.

SAND TARTS

"I want to have a good body,
but not as much as I want dessert."
Jason Love

These little sand tarts are also called Mexican wedding cookies. They're great for gatherings & office parties as long as no one cares if they're licking powdered sugar off their fingers.

Ingredients

4 ounces butter
1 cup nuts, chopped
¼ cup sugar
2 teaspoons vanilla
2 cups flour
powdered sugar

Instructions

Preheat oven to 375°F.

Mix all ingredients together. Spray a cookie sheet with nonstick cooking spray. Roll mixture into small balls & place on cookie sheet. Bake for 10 to 15 minutes. When done & slightly cooled, roll in powdered sugar. Roll again in powdered sugar after the cookies have cooled completely.

SHORTBREAD

"Cookies are made of butter & love."
Norwegian Proverb

Anything that involves vast quantities of butter puts a smile on my face. These are also easy to decorate. If you're baking for a special occasion, add colored frosting, toss with sprinkles, or follow your own sense of artistic expression.

Ingredients

4 cups flour, sifted
2 cups butter
1 cup sugar

Instructions

Combine all ingredients & knead by hand. Roll into logs & refrigerate until firm.

Preheat oven to 350°F.

Cut into ¼-inch thick cookie slices. Sprinkle lightly with sugar & bake for 10 to 12 minutes.

SWEET POTATO PIE

"Only a true Southern woman would turn a root vegetable into an irresistible dessert."
Elaine Acker

Yes, men bake too, & do a mighty fine job. But since Mama did the baking in our house, I'm honoring the ingenuity of southern women. Who needs pumpkins when you have sweet potatoes?

Ingredients:

1 pie crust (make Katherine's Best Pie Crust Ever or buy a pre-made crust from the store)
2 medium-size sweet potatoes
4 tablespoons butter
1 cup sugar
3 eggs
½ cup milk
1 ½ teaspoons vanilla
sprinkle cinnamon
pinch nutmeg

Instructions:

Preheat oven to 350°F.

Peel, cook, & mash the sweet potatoes to a smooth consistency. The potatoes can be cooked in water on the stove top or in a pressure cooker. Add all other ingredients & mix thoroughly. Pour into an unbaked, prepared pie crust. Bake for approximately one hour. Cool & serve with whipped cream (optional).

VANILLA CUSTARD

"There is no better way to bring people together than with desserts."

Gail Simmons

This recipe came from one of Mama's best friends, Dorothy Sayer. Mama made this recipe time after time & it reminds me of crème brulée (one of my personal favorites) & friendship.

Ingredients

3 eggs, beaten
1 ½ cups milk
⅓ cup sugar
1 teaspoon vanilla
sprinkle ground nutmeg

Instructions

Preheat oven to 325°F.

Combine all ingredients except nutmeg. Mix until well-combined but not frothy. Pour into four, 6-ounce custard cups. Place custard cups in a baking dish. Pour boiling water into the baking dish around the cups to a depth of about one inch. Bake for 30 to 45 minutes.

VANILLA BUTTERCREAM FROSTING

**"Eat butter first, & eat it last,
& live 'til a hundred years be past."**
Old Dutch Proverb

*I love any quote that encourages me to eat more butter.
My grandmother on my mother's side was Dutch. Hmm.*

Ingredients

6 tablespoons butter
2 cups powdered sugar
1 teaspoon vanilla
milk

Instructions

Mix all ingredients. Add milk one tablespoon at a time &
continue beating until the consistency is right.

MAMA'S HOMEMADE VANILLA ICE CREAM

"Always serve too much hot fudge sauce on hot fudge sundaes. It makes people overjoyed & puts them in your debt."

Judith Olney

Personally, I love homemade ice cream without the chocolate syrup or other toppings, with one notable exception. Try making the chocolate pie filling & drizzling it over a bowl of ice cream while the chocolate is still a little warm. It's life changing.

Ingredients

6 eggs
2 cups sugar
2 cans evaporated milk
2 tablespoons vanilla

Instructions

Pour mixture into the ice cream freezer. Add milk to the fill line. Freeze & enjoy! Makes 4 quarts. Feel free to add fresh, sweetened fruit. I highly recommend peaches.

ALL RECIPES INDEX

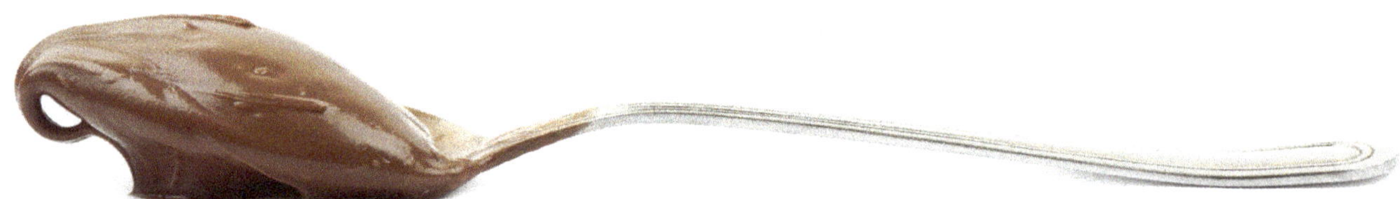

www.ingramcontent.com/pod-product-compliance
Lightning Source LLC
Chambersburg PA
CBHW040153110726
48005CB00018B/2739